MW0049O367

Cars with Fins

Cars with Fins

DIANE K. STEVENSON

ARIEL BOOKS

ANDREWS AND MCMEEL

KANSAS CITY

CARS WITH FINS

Photographs by Mike Mueller

ISBN: 0-8362-2642-9
Library of Congress Catalog Card Number: 96-85938

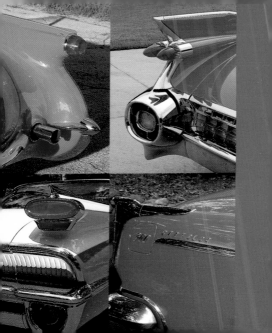

Contents

Nothing is more quintes-
sentially American than the
automobile; in fact, the automobile could be our national symbol
as easily as the eagle. And no era

is more representative of this
nation's enthusiastic, egalitarian
optimism than the 1950s: the
decade of cars with fins. Big as
boats, grandiose as floats in a
Mardi Gras parade, these power-
ful, flamboyant cars
captivated a country
in the middle of post-
war expansion and
economic prosperity.

It may come as a surprise that the car was not invented here in the New World, but in the Old. For centuries—beginning perhaps with Leonardo da Vinci's fifteenth-century sketches of a vehicle similar to the modern tank—there had been speculation about the possibilities of a self-propelled road machine. By the mid-nineteenth century, steam-powered omnibuses could be seen running up and down British streets. In the 1860s the French developed and patented the first internal combustion engine. Ten years later, the Americans joined the race and quickly took the lead.

Henry Ford's assembly line intro-
duced a crucial difference—it lowered
production costs so much that even the
ordinary man could afford a car. This was
the American contribution: a chicken in
every pot, a car in every garage. By 1908
the Model T was up and running and

there were nearly 400,000 cars bustling about on American roadways.

The first cars looked much like the horseless carriages they were replacing, but over time they became sleeker, faster, and more aerodynamic: true automobiles. For the most part, this evolution was pragmatic. Flights of design fancy were not allowed to mask basic function. While the fenders of early models, for example, may look stylized and attractive to us now, they served principally as protection for tires. For the time being, the aesthetic element remained subordinate.

OUT WITH THE OLD,
IN WITH THE FIN

*J*he defining characteristic of cars of the 1950s were the fins: Sharp or rounded, vertical or horizontal, chromed or painted, these fins brought to mind fish streamlined for water or jetliners streamlined for air. Yet neither sea nor sky is the medium for finned cars, whose tires

remain firmly planted on cement high-
ways or on asphalt roads. In fact, while
fins may conjure up notions of efficiency
and suggest maneuverability and speed,

they never served any such purpose; they were always mere ornament, mere embellishment, mere fantasy.

How did the whimsy and extrava-

gance of '50s car design come about? After all, the automobile is a straightforward piece of engineering. It has a practical purpose—to get its occupants where they are going as efficiently as possible. So why the frills and thrills?

Streamlining, the modern look of speed and efficiency, first appeared in the art deco style of the 1920s. But the boldness of this new design was kept in check, first by the depression and then by World War II. Nothing on a car was purely superfluous until the 1950s, when automobile design began to answer to a new master: the American consumer.

Emboldened by the postwar economic boom, consumers demanded style, comfort, and convenience; manufacturers,

recognizing a potentially huge market, turned their focus to innovative design.

The '50s was a decade with flair, not just in automobiles but in houses and in furniture, in toasters and in dinnerware. Everything—not just cars—looked like it was about to take off. Molded plastic, bent plywood, tubular metal: New materials inspired new styles. Fins were one of the multiple

appeals being made to the American consumer.

Automotively speaking, things were picking up. The 1950s saw the innovation of higher horsepower engines, automatic transmissions, power brakes, power steering, and

tubeless tires. This decade also saw the introduction of the taillight, the brake light, the back-up light, and the turn signal. Were the new fins needed to accommodate all these rear lights?

Not really. Fins were decorative and superfluous, an appeal to prestige. Cars were getting bigger and presumably better. They came in different styles, with hubcaps and chrome. They offered optional air-conditioning, heaters, and radios. They were available in different colors, two-tone and three-tone, their paint jobs so gleaming and reflective that some people considered them dangerous in traffic.

Here is a partial list of the options

and innovations newly available in those fabulous cars:

SWIVEL SEATS

ELECTRICAL SEAT ADJUSTMENT

SEAT BELTS

PADDED DASH PANELS

BACK-LIT INSTRUMENT PANELS

"SELF-WINDING" WATCHES AFFIXED TO THE STEERING WHEEL [EIGHT DAYS WITHOUT WINDING]

DUAL ILLUMINATED ASHTRAYS

PUSH-BUTTON AUTOMATIC TRANSMISSIONS

PUSH-BUTTON RADIOS

REAR SPEAKERS

NAUGAHYDE, VINYL, OR LEATHER INTERIORS

LINOLEUM FLOOR MATS

ELECTRICALLY

OPERATED

ANTENNAS

KEYLESS DOOR

LOCKS

CARPETED TRUNKS

COURTESY LIGHTS

LICENSE PLATE

LAMPS

FOG AND DRIVING

LIGHTS

HOODED HEADLIGHTS

CHROMED HEADLIGHT SURROUNDS

TINTED GREEN GLASS

WRAPAROUND WINDOWS

WINDSHIELD WIPERS

WRAPAROUND CHROMED GRILLES

REMOVABLE ROOF PANELS

TWO-TONE SIDE PANELING

REAR FENDER SKIRTS

WHITEWALL TIRES

WIRE WHEEL COVERS

FAKE SPARE TIRE MOUNTS ON REAR DECKS

DUAL FUEL TANKS

A PARADE OF CLASSICS

*T*oday, the distinctive style of the fabulous '50s is decidedly collectible, perhaps because we are nostalgic for a more unequivocally idealistic period when people looked to the future with optimism and progress was not yet a discredited word. Nothing since has rivaled the outrageous flair of cars with fins— they are a lost national art. The following pages give you just a hint of the grandeur of their once uncontested supremacy— like the mighty dinosaurs of an earlier age.

1953 NASH-HEALEY

1954 KAISER-DARRIN

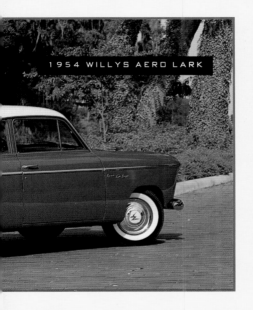

1954 WILLYS AERO LARK

1955
MERCURY
MONTCLAIR
SUN VALLEY

1955 CORVETTE

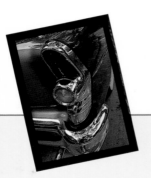

1955 BUICK
CENTURY

1955 CHRYSLER
C-300

1955 FORD
VICTORIA

1955 PACKARD CARIBBEAN

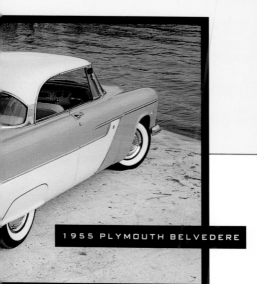

1955 PLYMOUTH BELVEDERE

1956 DODGE
CUSTOM ROYAL
LANCER D-500

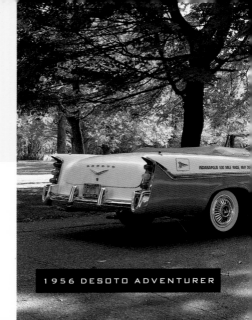

1956 DESOTO ADVENTURER

DE SOTO

Official
PACE CAR

1956 PLYMOUTH FURY

1957 STUDEBAKER
GOLDEN HAWK

1957 PONTIAC STAR CHIEF TRI-POWER

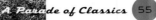

1957 CHRYSLER
300C

1957 CHEVROLET
BEL AIR

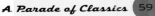

1957 FORD
RANCHERO

1957 CHEVROLET NOMAD

1957 FORD
THUNDERBIRD

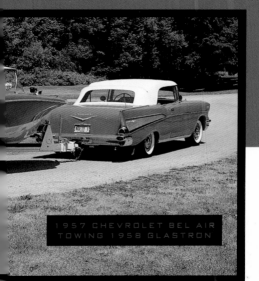

1957 CHEVROLET BEL AIR
TOWING 1958 GLASTRON

1958 CONTINENTAL
MARK III

1958 PLYMOUTH FURY

1959 CADILLAC
SERIES 62

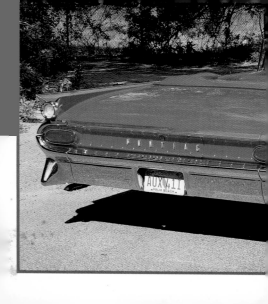

1959 PONTIAC CATALINA

1959 OLDSMOBILE

1959 CHEVROLET IMPALA

1959 CHEVROLET IMPALA

This book was set in Bauer Bodoni, Banque, and Fleece.

Book design and typesetting by

JUDITH STAGNITTO ABBATE